THE SUPER SCIENCE BOOK OF SOUND

David Glover

SOUNDS FOR MYSELF

I would like
To pin sound
To the ground –
To catch
And keep –
To let loose
When I choose
To use
It.

Belching frogs
And barking dogs

Babbly brooks
And whispering books

Porcelain smashing
And cymbals kerrashing

Buzzy bees
And squally seas

These are the sounds for myself,

The ones I'd like to keep
For me
To set free
When I just
Want to listen.

BY LIZZIE LEWIS

Illustrations by Frances Lloyd

Thomson Learning

New York

Books in the Super Science series

Energy	**Our Bodies**
The Environment	**Sound**
Forces	**Space**
Light	**Time**
Materials	**Weather**

First published in the
United States in 1994 by
Thomson Learning
115 Fifth Avenue
New York, NY 10003

First published in 1994 by
Wayland (Publishers) Ltd.

UK version copyright © 1994 Wayland (Publishers) Ltd.

U.S. version copyright © 1994 Thomson Learning

Sounds For Myself copyright © 1993 Liz Lewis

Library of Congress Cataloging-in-Publication Data
Glover, David.
　The super science book of sound / David Glover ;
illustrations by Frances Lloyd.
　　　　p.　　　cm.—(Super science)
　Includes bibliographical references and index.
　ISBN: 1-56847-156-4 : $14.95
　1. Sound—Juvenile literature. [1. Sound.] I. Lloyd,
Frances, ill. II. Title. III. Series.
QC225.5.G56　　1994
534—dc20　　　　　　　　　　　　　　93-41693

Printed in Italy

Series Editor: James Kerr
Designer: Loraine Hayes Design

Picture acknowledgments

Illustrations by Frances Lloyd.
Cover illustration by Martin Gordon.

Photographs by permission of: Camera Press 13, 15, 27; Eye Ubiquitous 25; Michael Holford 23 (top); Oxford Scientific Films 17, 20 (left), 21; Photri Inc. 12, 16, 19, 22; Tony Stone Worldwide 5, 6, 7, 10, 11, 20 (MacNeal Hospital, right), 23 (bottom); Topham Picture Source 26; Wayland Picture Library 8; Zefa 24; World in the Park Ltd. 28; Zul 9.

CONTENTS

Surrounded by Sound 4
Sounds in the Night 5
Sound Waves 6
The Sound of Silence 7
High and Low 8
Loud and Soft 9
Sound Barrier 10
Sound Energy 11
Echoes 12
Voices 13
Listening Ear 14
Silent World 15
Heartbeat 16
Big Ears 17
Down in the Jungle 18
Dawn Chorus 19
Ultrasound 20
Underwater Sound 21
The Sound of Music 22
Musical Instruments 23
Blow Your Own Trumpet 24
Rhythms of the World 25
Electronic Sounds 26
Recorded Sound 27
Sound Studio 28
Sound Communications 29

Glossary 30
Books to Read 31
Index 32

SURROUNDED BY SOUND

The world is full of sound. Shut your eyes and listen for a moment. Some sounds are natural, such as the wind in the trees, the patter of falling rain, or the calls of animals in the country. Where there are people, there are the sounds of voices, music, and laughter. In towns and cities, most of the sounds we hear are made by machines. The air is filled with the roar of traffic, the rumble of passing trains, and noises from construction sites and factories.

Can you shut your eyes and tell where you are, just by listening to sounds? It's fairly easy to tell if you are in the town or country. But which sounds prove you are in a friend's house instead of your own? Even a small sound like a door squeaking or a floorboard creaking might give you a clue.

We ignore some sounds and listen carefully to others. Sounds can warn us of danger, entertain us, soothe us, and wake us up. One important way we use sound is to communicate by talking to one another.

SOUNDS IN THE NIGHT

Do you ever lie awake at night listening to sounds around your house? Even in the country it's never completely quiet. A clock ticks, a car passes, a dog barks, a faucet drips. If nothing else, you can always hear the sound of your own breathing.

Which of these sounds can you hear from your bedroom at night?

A ticking clock

Traffic

Trains

Airplanes

People

Animals

Try counting the different sounds you hear before falling asleep, instead of counting sheep!

Animals that hunt at night use sound to call to each other and to find their prey. Foxes have sharp hearing to listen for voles and other small animals scurrying through the underbrush. An owl sometimes hoots for the same reason that a wolf sometimes howls: to warn rivals to stay out of its territory. When it hunts, the owl flies silently, giving no warning as it swoops down with talons outstretched.

SOUND WAVES

◀ Sounds travel through the air as waves, like water waves spreading when a stone is thrown into a pond. Sound waves are made by vibrations pushing the air back and forth.

When you hit a drum the skin vibrates up and down very quickly (too fast to see), making the air above it vibrate as well. The vibrating air pushes on the air surrounding it, which pushes on more air, passing on the vibrations to your ears.

You can feel vibrations when you stroke a purring cat or touch a ringing telephone. Try holding your hand against your throat to feel the vibrations when you speak or sing. If you want to see vibrations, then sprinkle some grains of rice on a sheet of paper and lay it on top of a radio or a loudspeaker. Turn up the volume and watch the rice dance! ▼

Sound waves travel through the air, through the ground, and through water. The molecules, or tiny particles, in solids (such as packed earth or wood) and liquids (such as water) are much closer together than the particles in air, so they pass on sound vibrations more quickly than air does.

WOW!
Sound travels four to five times faster through water and more than fifteen times faster through steel than it does through the air!

THE SOUND OF
SILENCE

◀ Where can you go for perfect peace and quiet? Try a trip into space. There is no air in space, so there is nothing to pass on sound vibrations. Sound waves can only travel where there are solids, liquids, or gases (such as air) to carry them. The only sounds a space-walking astronaut can hear are those inside his or her spacesuit, which contains air.

By 1660, scientist Robert Boyle had proved that sound cannot pass through empty space. He placed a watch with a loud tick inside a glass jar and slowly pumped out the air. The tick became quieter and quieter until it could not be heard at all. When Boyle let the air back into the jar he could hear the tick again. ▶

WOW!
Rockets, which are so noisy on earth that they can damage your ears, are completely silent in space. There is no air in space to carry sound.

HIGH AND LOW

Have you ever covered your ears when you heard an ear-piercing whistle? Have you been in a building and felt it shake as a big truck passed by? A whistle is a high-pitched sound, as is a squeak or a scream. The rumble of a truck is a low-pitched sound, as is a bear's growl or a roll of thunder. Loud, high-pitched sounds hurt your ears. Loud, low-pitched sounds vibrate through your body; you feel them in the pit of your stomach. Loud, low-pitched sounds rattle doors and windows, and can even damage buildings.

◀ The difference between high- and low-pitched sounds is the rate, or frequency, of vibration. High-pitched sounds are made by rapid vibrations; low-pitched sounds are made by slow vibrations. Most things have a natural frequency at which they vibrate. A small instrument makes a higher-pitched sound than a big one, because small, light things vibrate more quickly than large, heavy ones.

You can make sounds with different ▶ pitches by holding a ruler over the edge of a table and flicking the end to make it vibrate. How does the pitch change when you change the length of the vibrating section?

8

LOUD AND SOFT

Turning up the volume on a TV or CD ▶ player doesn't change the pitch of the sound. It just makes the vibrations bigger, so that the sound is louder. The size of the vibrations is called the amplitude of a sound wave. The bigger the amplitude, the louder the sound.

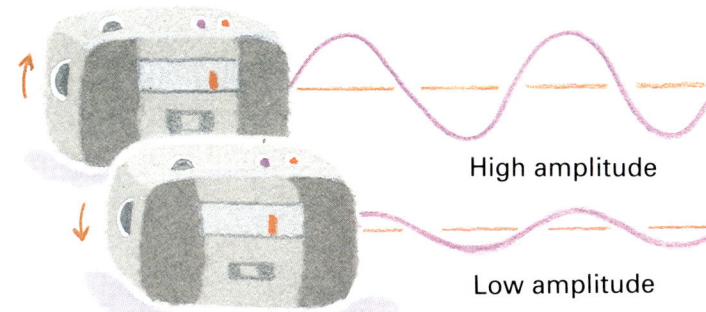

The loudness of a sound is measured in decibels. The sound of a falling leaf is 0 decibels; whispering, 10 decibels; talking, 30–60 decibels; loud rock music, 90–120 decibels. Sounds over 110 decibels are so loud they can hurt your ears.

▲ Sometimes sound can be a kind of pollution. Loud sounds are annoying and can be dangerous. It can even be dangerous to play a personal stereo too loudly. All the sound goes straight into your ears and even though it may not hurt at the time, if the sound is too loud it may lead to hearing loss. People who work in very noisy places must wear ear protectors so that their hearing is not damaged.

"It was so quiet you could hear a pin drop" is a well-known saying. Can you hear a pin drop? See if you can hear a pin fall onto different surfaces from various heights. What happens when you increase the height? On which surface does the falling pin make the most noise?

9

SOUND BARRIER

How fast does sound travel?

In a thunderstorm you ▶ always hear the crack of thunder after you see the flash of lightning. The light reaches your eyes almost instantly, but sound takes about five seconds to travel one mile through air. You can judge how far away a storm is by timing the interval between the flash and the crash. Five seconds and the storm is one mile away; ten seconds, two miles – and so on.

At room temperature, the speed of sound through air is about 1,100 feet per second or about 750 miles per hour. When an airplane flies at this speed you cannot hear it coming because it keeps up with the sounds it makes. When it goes faster, it overtakes the sound, breaking the sound barrier. On the ground, the sound arrives after the aircraft has passed, causing a loud bang called a sonic boom.

The first scientist to study sonic booms ▶ was Austrian Ernst Mach. Today the speeds of jets are often given as Mach numbers. The speed of sound is Mach 1. The Concorde can fly at Mach 2, which is twice the speed of sound. The world air speed record is held by a Lockheed SR-71A jet, which flew at Mach 3.5 near the Beale Air Force base in California on July 28, 1976.

10

SOUND ENERGY

Like heat and light, sound is a form of energy. Sonic booms, explosions, and other sudden loud sounds carry huge amounts of power. A powerful boom travels through the air like a tidal wave across the sea. It can knock people over, shatter windows, and even destroy buildings.

WOW!
When the volcanic island of Krakatoa exploded in 1883, the noise was heard more than 2,500 miles away. It was one of the loudest sounds ever heard on earth.

If you blow up a paper bag and burst it between your hands, the energy you use by squeezing the air in the bag is released with a bang when the bag splits. Tires and balloons also burst with a bang if they are punctured suddenly.

Make a sound cannon

1. Stretch sheets of plastic over the ends of a cardboard tube and tape them tightly in place.
2. Make a small hole, a little bigger than a pinhole, in the center of the plastic at one end.
3. Hold the sound cannon so that the hole is near a pinch of powdered sugar. Tap the other end of the cannon.

The sound energy from the tube blows the sugar across the table. You can also use the cannon to make ripples on a bowl of water.

ECHOES
ECHOES
ECHOES

Have you ever stood near a cliff or in a large empty building and clapped or shouted to hear the echo? Just as light is reflected by mirrors, sounds are reflected from hard surfaces like walls and rocks. An echo is a sound reflection.

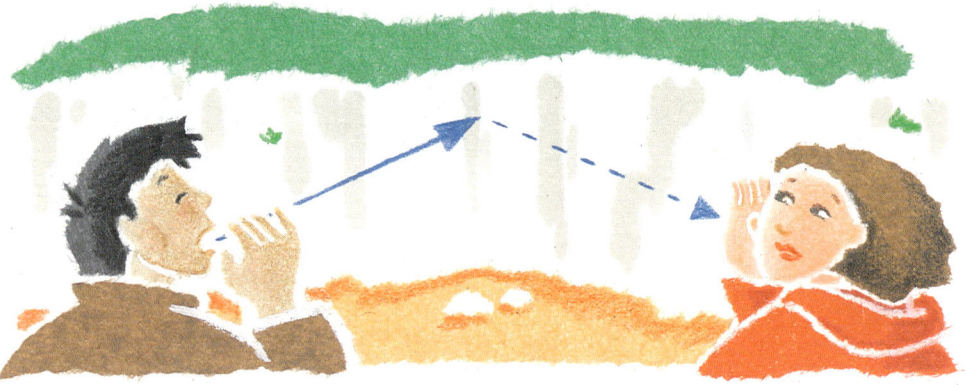

When the sound of your voice bounces back from a cliff, you hear a single echo. In a tunnel or under a bridge you may hear a whole series of echoes as the sound bounces around. Echoes arriving rapidly one after another is called reverberation.

▲ Sailors in a fog used to judge the distance to dangerous cliffs by sounding a foghorn. By timing the echo and knowing the speed of sound, they could calculate the distance to the cliffs.

Alpine horns were ▶ developed by people living in mountainous countries such as Switzerland. A loud noise is made by blowing the horn. The sound is reflected by lakes and mountain-sides, and the echoes can be heard several miles away. Alpine horns were used to send simple messages.

VOICES

We use our voices to talk, shout, and sing by making the vocal chords in our throat vibrate with air from our lungs. To change the sound, we tighten our throat muscles and change the shape of our mouth and lips.

Say the vowel sounds a, e, i, o, u. You can feel how the sounds from your throat are shaped by your mouth. Now say the consonants: sounds such as s, b, and p made without a vowel sound (say "sss," "b," and "p," not "ess," "bee," and "pee"). Consonant sounds are made more with your lips and tongue than with your throat. Can you sing vowels? What about consonants?

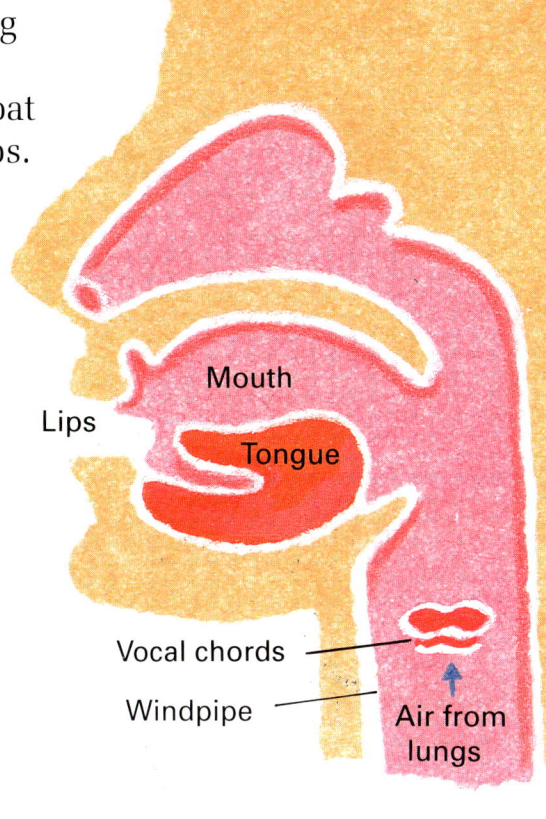

◀ All human voices change with age. Boys' voices break when they are 12 to 15 years old, changing from high-pitched to low-pitched. Opera singers train their voices for years until they become incredibly powerful. A trained singer can break a wineglass by singing a note that exactly matches the vibration frequency of the glass. The sound energy causes the glass to vibrate so much that it shatters.

WOW! Simon Robinson made the loudest scream ever measured. In the Guinness Challenge on November 11, 1988, his scream was recorded at 128 decibels!

LISTENING EAR

Human ears are incredibly sensitive. The quietest sound we can detect is more than a billion times softer than a noisy heavy metal group. Ears are also very delicate.

▶ Inside the ear is a piece of skin stretched like a taut drumskin, called the eardrum. Sound waves make the eardrums vibrate. The vibrations are passed on by tiny bones called the hammer, anvil, and stirrup (the smallest bones in the human body) to the inner ear. In the inner ear, the vibrations cause nerves to send signals to the brain. You must never push anything into your ears – you could easily puncture an eardrum and make yourself deaf.

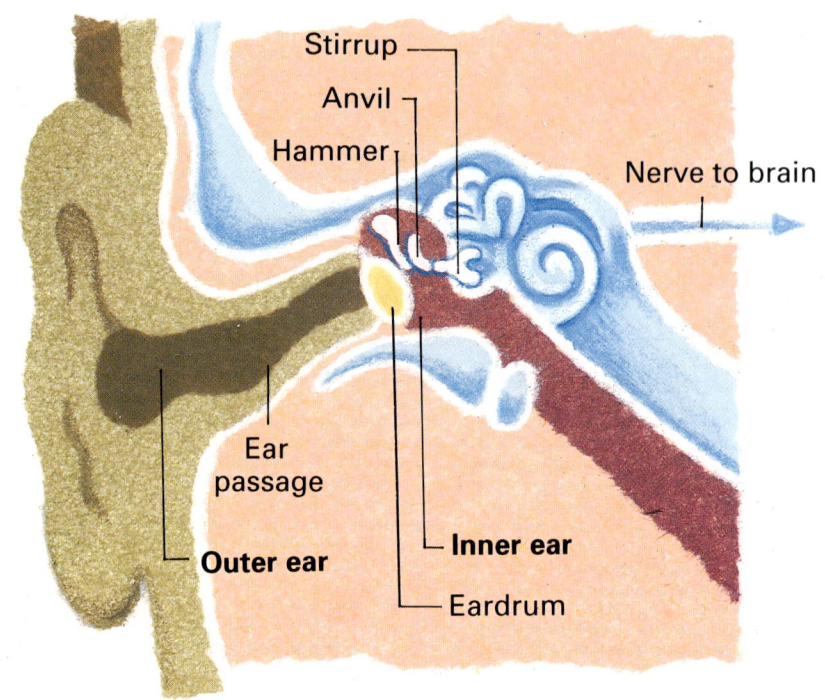

Why do we have two ears? One reason is that a sound from the right of our body reaches the right ear just a fraction of a second before it reaches the left ear. Our brain can use this information to decide where the sound is coming from.

▶ Can you tell which direction sounds come from when you are blindfolded? Ask a friend to blindfold you and to make sounds from different parts of the room. Can you point toward the sound? Is it easier with a high-pitched sound or a low-pitched one? Is it more difficult if you cover one ear?

SILENT WORLD

Evelyn Glennie is deaf, ▶ yet she is a world-famous musician. Although she cannot hear the drums and other percussion instruments she plays, she can feel their vibrations with her hands and the rest of her body.

People who are completely deaf can communicate by reading lips and using sign language. Many deaf children learn to speak by copying the mouth and lip movements they see. In one form of sign language, the hands form shapes to represent letters. Another type of sign language, the American Sign Language, is based on concepts rather than words.

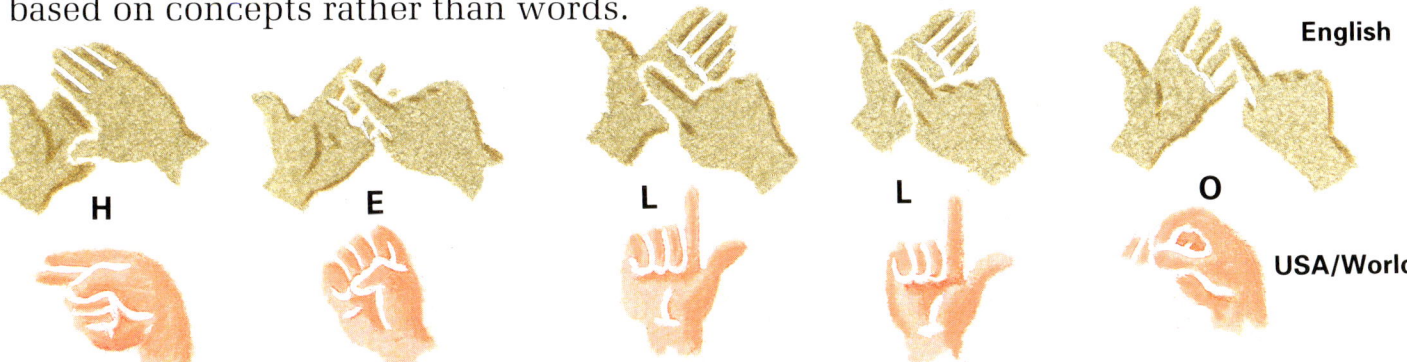

English

H E L L O

USA/World

Hearing aids help people who are partly deaf. ▶ Perhaps their ears have been damaged by an accident or by an illness. People often become hard of hearing as they get older, when the bones and nerves in the ears stop working properly. Victorian ear trumpets worked by collecting sounds and concentrating them into a conical tube held against the ear. Modern hearing aids have tiny electronic amplifiers, similar to but much smaller than the amplifier in a stereo system. A microphone picks up the sound and the amplifier makes it louder as it enters the ear.

HEARTBEAT

A stethoscope carries the sounds of ▶ your body along hollow plastic tubes to a doctor's ears. The regular rhythm of your heartbeat shows that you are alive and well. The doctor also listens to your breathing to check that your lungs are working properly.

Testing Stethoscopes

Find out which of these two stethoscopes is better for listening to different kinds of sounds.

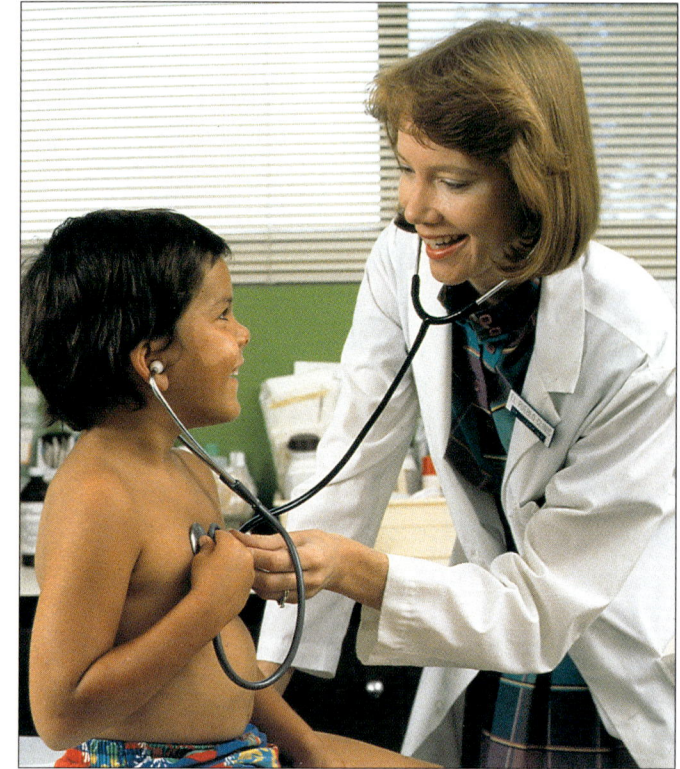

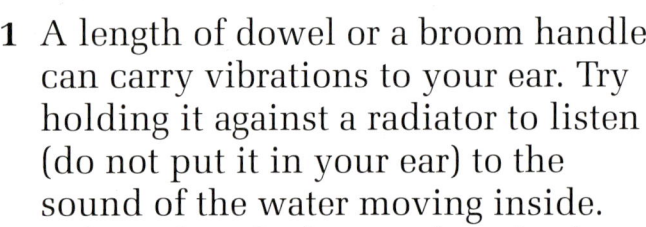

1. A length of dowel or a broom handle can carry vibrations to your ear. Try holding it against a radiator to listen (do not put it in your ear) to the sound of the water moving inside.
2. A funnel pushed into a length of hose collects sounds in the same way as an ear trumpet.

Try listening to a ticking watch. With funnels at both ends of the tube, you have an intercom. How can you make your test fair? To compare two stethoscopes, listen to the same things with each one.

Car mechanics know that when an engine is running well it sounds smooth and quiet. Loud knocking or squealing means something is wrong. A wooden listening-stick or a stethoscope helps the mechanic to find the problem.

BIG EARS

Many animals have hearing that is more sensitive than that of humans. Sound is a good way for them to find food and detect danger. Rabbits can move their ears separately to listen for danger signals from different directions. If they are alarmed, they sound a warning by thumping the ground with their back legs.

Can you hear an ant ▶ walking underground? Aardvarks can. They use their long, sensitive ears to listen for ants and termites moving in their nests. Then they dig down with their strong front claws and lick them up.

Elephants have the biggest ears in the animal kingdom. But they are not shaped for hearing. In fact, they help the elephant keep its huge body cool. Heat escapes from the elephant's blood as it flows through the ears, close to the skin's surface.

Ear shapes

What is the best shape for an ear? Test ear trumpets of different shapes made from thin cardboard. Which shape is best for listening to very quiet sounds? Which shape is best for telling the direction from which a sound is coming?

DOWN IN THE JUNGLE

Some of the noisiest animals in the world live in the rain forest. Parrots screech, frogs croak, monkeys howl and scream.

Even when the larger jungle animals fall silent there is still a constant hum made by millions of insects. Insects don't have lungs like mammals, birds, and reptiles, so they can't make sounds by forcing air from their mouths. They make noises by clicking and scraping the hard outer parts of their bodies. Bees buzz because their wings beat so quickly. Grasshoppers scrape a comb of stiff hairs on their legs to make chirping noises. Bombardier beetles can squirt a puff of gas that explodes with a loud pop to frighten away a predator.

Animal sounds are not just noise. They are usually messages with a purpose. A family of gibbons moving through the jungle trees keeps in touch with calls that can mean anything from "watch out, there is an eagle above" to "here is something good to eat."

WOW!
Howler monkeys make the loudest sounds of any land animals. Their howls can be heard more than 10 miles away!

DAWN CHORUS

As the sun begins to rise, birds wake up and sing loudly. The dawn chorus greets the start of a new day. Ornithologists study birdsong by recording and displaying the sounds on graphs. These show the different frequencies and amplitudes for each particular birdsong. Like other animals, birds use sound to communicate with one another, and with other species.

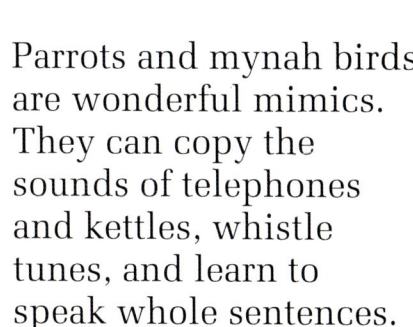

Sound print

When the male North American sage grouse is courting, he puffs up air sacs on his neck and makes a popping sound. The ruffed grouse has a different style: he makes a drumming sound by vibrating the air with his wings. The common loon, which lives in North America, makes a call at night that sounds like mad laughter. ▼

Parrots and mynah birds are wonderful mimics. They can copy the sounds of telephones and kettles, whistle tunes, and learn to speak whole sentences.

The scaly-throated honey guide chatters to draw the attention of a person or a badger to a bees' nest. The bird is not able to open the nest itself, but when the nest is opened by a bigger animal the guide is rewarded with a share of the honey.

WOW! An African gray parrot called Prudle learned to say nearly 800 different words!

ULTRASOUND

Not only can many animals hear quieter sounds than can human beings, they also hear higher-pitched sounds. Scientists use the words ultrasonic and ultrasound to describe high-pitched noise vibrations beyond the range of human hearing. Dogs and cats are sensitive to ultrasound. Some dog whistles seem silent when blown, but they make a very high-pitched sound that human ears cannot hear.

Bats make ultrasonic squeaks and listen for their echoes to find moths in the dark. But the moths are alert to the danger. They are sensitive to ultrasound and, if they are quick enough, they can swerve to escape. Some moths can even squeak back to confuse the bat. ▼

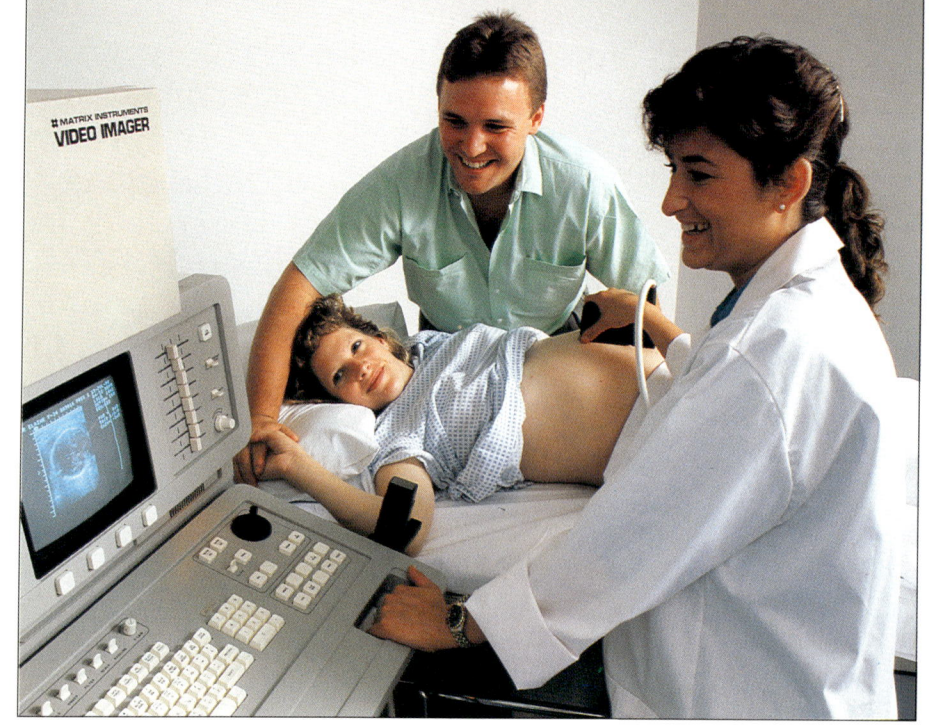

▲ Although we cannot hear ultrasound, we can still make use of it. This picture of an unborn baby in its mother's uterus was made with ultrasound echoes. The doctor holds a scanner, which sends ultrasonic waves into the uterus, over the mother's body. The echoes are measured and displayed on a computer screen, making a picture of the baby. The doctor can check if it is healthy without harming the patients.

UNDERWATER SOUND

From dry land the underwater world ▶ looks silent, but it is full of sound. Sounds travel well through water. The beautiful, eerie songs of the great whales travel for hundreds of miles through the oceans. Whales may sing for hours at a time and they are clearly communicating with one another, but we can only guess at the meaning of the sounds they make.

◀ Dolphins use echoes underwater in a similar way to bats. The rare river dolphins that live in the Yangtze in China and in some rivers in India are almost blind. So little light penetrates the murky waters of these great rivers that the dolphins' eyes have become weak and tiny. They depend almost completely on sound to find fish and to swim safely through the water.

On her maiden voyage in 1912, the luxury liner *Titanic* struck an iceberg and sank with the loss of more than 1,000 lives. This terrible disaster led French scientist Paul Langevin to develop a sonar system. The sonar system sends sound pulses into the water and detects echoes. The strength and direction of the echoes give information about objects beneath the surface. Today, sonar is used by many vessels to measure the depth of the sea, to find wrecks, to locate schools of fish, and to detect submarines.

THE SOUND OF MUSIC

Whales and birds sing – and so do humans. The sound of music can excite us, make us feel happy or sad, soothe or calm us. It's difficult to say exactly what music is, since there are so many different kinds. Some people's music sounds like just noise to others. But music can be almost any sound that people make to express their feelings and entertain each other.

Musical sounds are written down as notes. Each note is a sound with a certain pitch and length. A musical scale is a series of notes of increasing pitch that seem to follow each other in a pleasing way. The first scale that most people living in western countries learn is the tonic sol-fa: doh, ray, me, fah, soh, lah, te, doh.

Many musical instruments – for example, a recorder or a trumpet – play a single note at a time. Others, such as pianos and guitars, can play several notes together. If the notes seem to fit together well they are called a chord. If the notes seem to clash and sound unpleasant together, the result is called discord.

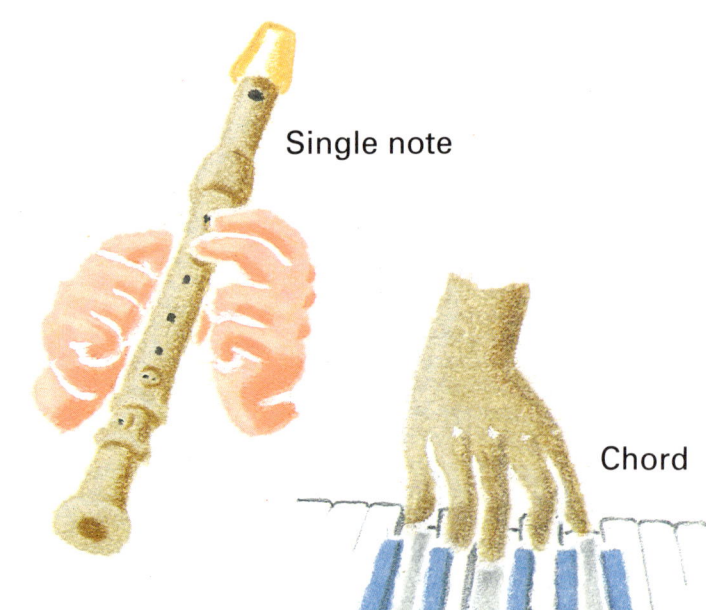

Single note

Chord

MUSICAL INSTRUMENTS

◀ No one knows when or how the first musical instruments were invented, but people have been making music for thousands of years. Whistles made from animal bones more than 25,000 years ago have been found in Hungary. Egyptian tomb paintings show harps and flutes. This harp was found buried with the pharaoh Ariv. It is more than 3,000 years old.

Today there are hundreds of different kinds of instruments. Although instruments come in many shapes and sizes there are just three basic types: strings, wind, and percussion. String instruments make sounds when a taut string is plucked or scraped; wind sounds are made by blowing into a tube to make the air inside vibrate; percussion instruments are played by hitting or tapping something solid to make it vibrate.

The strings on this instrument, a ▶ ravanhatta, are tuned by turning pegs to alter their tension. The musician makes different notes by pressing the strings against frets to shorten the lengths of the strings. The shorter the string, the higher the pitch. The strings are played by rubbing them with a bow. The vibrations of the strings make the air inside the small sound box vibrate too, increasing the volume of sound.

BLOW YOUR OWN TRUMPET

If you blow sharply across the open end of a pen top it makes a high-pitched whistle. Blowing across the mouth of an empty bottle makes a lower-pitched sound because the vibrating air column inside is longer. This is how panpipes work. Each pipe makes a different note. The shorter pipes make higher-pitched notes than the longer ones.

A saxophone player plays different notes by pressing keys to open and close holes in the tube of his or her instrument. Opening a hole has the same effect as shortening the tube, which raises the pitch of the note. The sound is made by blowing over a reed in the mouthpiece. The reed vibrates like vocal chords, which makes the air inside the saxophone vibrate.

Didgeridoos are hollow wooden pipes. ▶ The aboriginal people in Australia have made them for thousands of years. When the player vibrates his or her lips (like blowing a raspberry) at the end of the tube it makes a low growling sound. Long cardboard tubes make excellent didgeridoos. Compare the sounds you can make with tubes of different lengths.

WOW!
The largest and loudest musical instrument in the world was an organ in Atlantic City, New Jersey, which could make a sound as loud as 25 brass bands.

RHYTHMS OF THE WORLD

At carnival time, bands of musicians beat out lively dance rhythms as they parade in their fabulous costumes. Almost anything can be used as a percussion instrument to tap out a beat: cans, sticks, bottles, and pans are all put to work. Rhythm gives music pattern and mood. A fast rhythm is lively and makes you want to dance. Slow rhythms are calmer and more relaxing.

Some percussion instruments are tuned to play different notes. A steel band plays its bright melodies on instruments made from old oil drums. Each different-sized panel, beaten into the top of the drum, makes a different note when tapped.

◀ An Indonesian gamelan orchestra hits a variety of gongs, tuned to different notes, with mallets.

Tap a tune

Make your own musical instrument by ▶ hanging various-sized tin lids, spoons, nails, and keys from a string tied between two chairs. Arrange the items so they are in order of increasing pitch. Can you find enough objects to make a complete scale, so that you can tap out tunes?

ELECTRONIC SOUNDS

In 1820, Hans Christian Oersted discovered that a wire carrying an electric current is moved by a force when it is put near a magnet. Not only did this discovery lead Michael Faraday to invent the electric motor, but it also led to the invention of the loudspeaker. Today's radios, television sets, stereo systems, and electronic musical instruments all use loudspeakers to reproduce sounds.

Inside a loudspeaker there is a coil of wire and a magnet. The coil is fixed to a cardboard cone. When an electric current flows in the coil the magnetic force makes the cone vibrate, sending out sound waves.▼

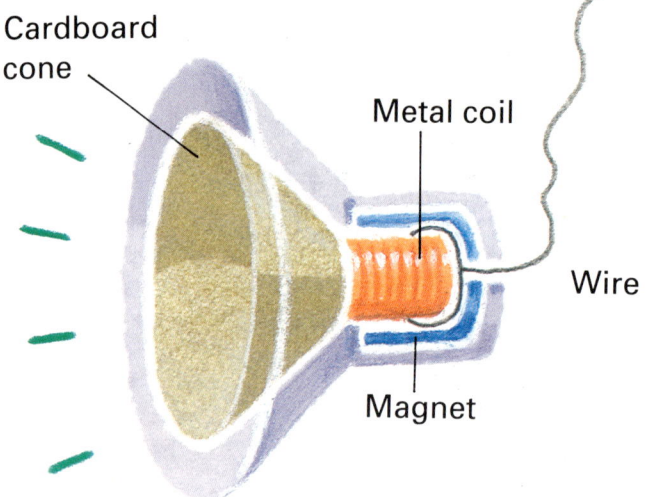

Cardboard cone
Metal coil
Wire
Magnet

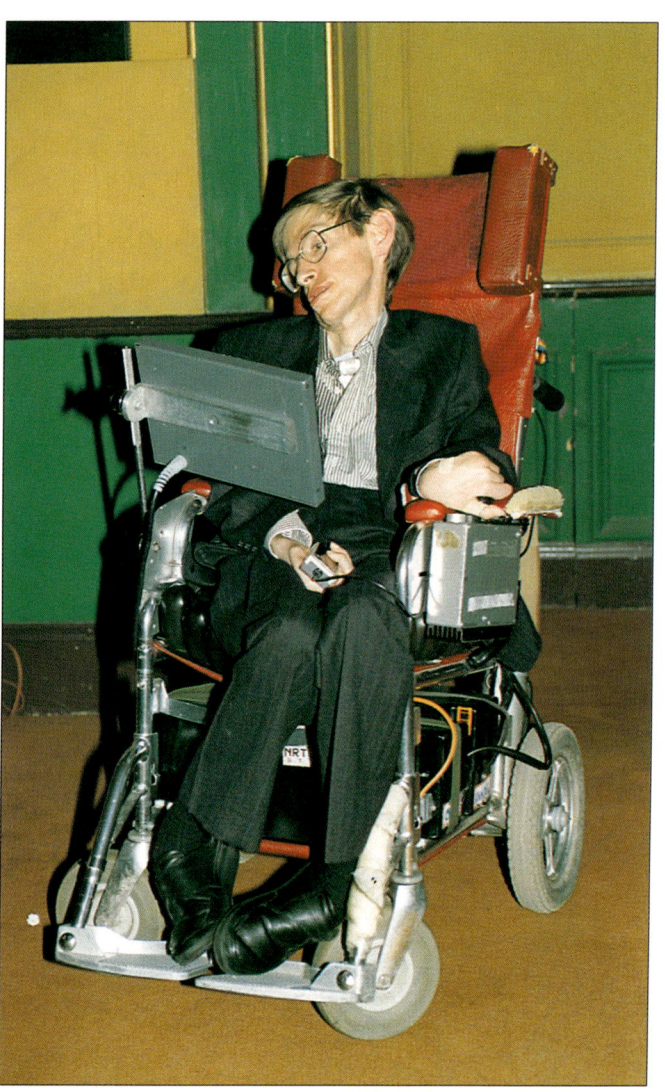

◀ A synthesizer or electronic keyboard is connected to a loudspeaker by an amplifier. Computer chips in the synthesizer are programmed to make electric patterns or signals the same shape as the sound waves made by other musical instruments. The amplifier increases the power of the signal and feeds it into the loudspeaker to make sounds. A synthesizer can mimic the sound of any musical instrument. It can even imitate the human voice. People who are unable to speak themselves, like the scientist Stephen Hawking (pictured here), can talk with the aid of a speech synthesizer.

RECORDED SOUND

◀ "Mary had a little lamb whose fleece was white as snow…" In 1879 Thomas Edison, the great American inventor, spoke these words into his phonograph to make the first-ever sound recording. The sound waves from Edison's voice made a needle vibrate, cutting a wavy, continuous groove in a spinning wax cylinder. The sound was played back by turning the cylinder so that the needle followed the groove, making it vibrate in just the same pattern.

Modern long-playing records, called LPs, work in the same way. The tiny vibrations of the needle are amplified electronically and fed to a loudspeaker.

Cassette tapes record sound waves as magnetic patterns on a strip of magnetic tape.

WOW! There are more than 500,000,000 numbers on one compact disc!

Records and cassettes are called ▶ analog sound recordings. This means that the sound pattern is copied as closely as possible in the record groove or on the tape. A digital recording uses a different method. Computer chips turn the sound into a list of numbers or digits, which are stored on a compact disc or a digital tape. When the recording is played back the numbers are read and used to recreate the sound wave almost exactly.

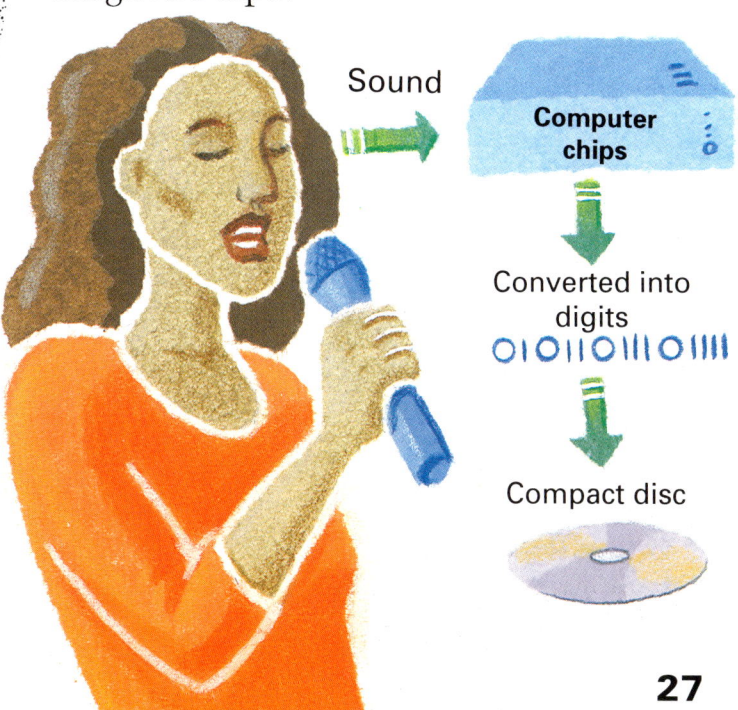

27

SOUND STUDIO

When a musical group makes a record the musicians play their instruments and sing into microphones. They don't have to play all at once. The recording engineer can mix sounds together to build up the recording in layers, like a collage on paper.

A recording studio is ▶ packed with computers, keyboards, amplifiers, loudspeakers, tape machines – everything needed to produce any possible sound.

▲ Keyboards called samplers make new sounds from old ones. A sampler can take a sound – for example, a door slamming or a sheep bleating – and play it back at a different speed or pitch. It can also add echoes and can even play the sound backwards. Using samplers, sounds from old recordings are reused to make new recordings that sound quite different.

Try making your own sound samples with a cassette recorder around your home or at school. You could use the sounds as effects for a school play. Try mimicking sounds to create special effects: use coconut shells to make the sounds of a horse's hooves, or shout into a bucket to make it sound as if you have fallen down a well.

SOUND COMMUNICATIONS

Throughout history, certain sounds have been used as signals. Church bells ring to call people to the service. Ambulances and fire engines sound sirens to warn that they are rushing to an emergency.

Normally the sound of our voices carries no more than a few hundred yards. To send messages over long distances requires electricity. In the last century, messages were sent along telegraph wires as a series of short and long beeps called Morse code.

The telephone converts the vibrations of air made by our voices into electrical impulses, which can be sent anywhere in the world. The ring of the telephone tells us that someone wishes to speak to us. ▼

How will we use sound in the future? Talking computers already exist. Talking machines will soon be common: microwave ovens will tell us when our dinner is ready; bathroom scales will tell us if we have gained weight. It will not be many years before computers that understand speech become common. In the future, instead of pressing a button to turn off the light and play a CD we will simply say: "Lights off, start the music," and our favorite sounds will fill the darkened room.

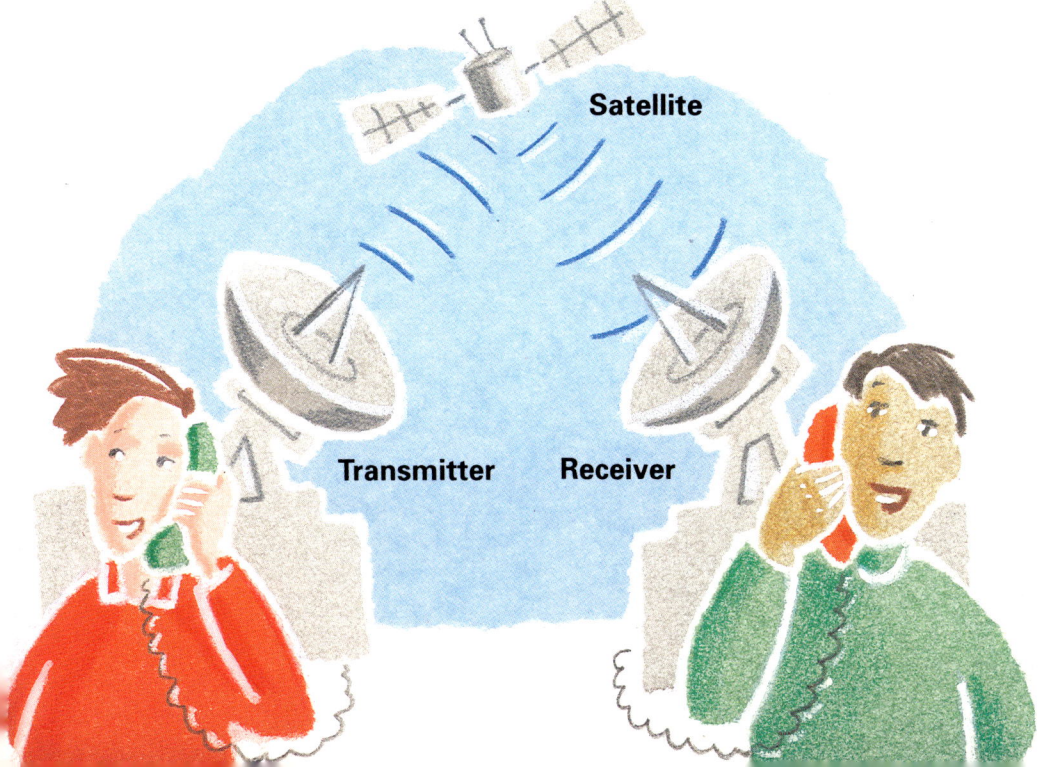

29

GLOSSARY

Amplifier An electronic device that increases the power of a sound.
Amplitude The size of a vibration or the height of a wave.
Analog recording A sound recording in the form of a wavy groove in a record or a magnetic pattern on tape.
Billion One thousand million, written as 1,000,000,000.
Decibel A measure of loudness.
Digital recording A sound recording as a series of numbers on a compact disc or a digital tape.
Echo A sound reflection.
Frequency The rate or speed of a vibration.
Loudspeaker A device that turns electrical signals into sound waves.
Mach number A measure of speed in terms of the speed of sound.
Microphone A device that turns sound waves into electrical signals.
Ornithologist Person who studies birds.
Percussion instrument A musical instrument played by hitting or tapping.
Pitch A musical term for the frequency of a sound.
Reverberation The sound of echoes in a cave or a large empty building.
Sampler An electronic keyboard that can record sounds and play them back at different pitches.
Sonar A device carried by ships to locate objects underwater by using sound echoes.
Sonic boom The sound made by an aircraft when it breaks the sound barrier.
Sound barrier A sudden large increase in air pressure on an aircraft as it approaches the speed of sound.
Sound wave A wave of vibration carrying sound energy through a solid, a liquid, or a gas.
Stethoscope An instrument used by a doctor to listen to sounds inside the body.
Synthesizer An electronic instrument that can mimic the sounds made by other instruments.
Ultrasound Very high-pitched sound beyond the range of human hearing.
Vibration A rapid back-and-forth movement.

BOOKS TO READ

Berger, Melvin. *The Science of Music.* New York: HarperCollins Children's Books, 1989.

Cash, Terry. *Sound.* Fun With Science. New York: Warwick Press, 1989.

Friedhoffer, Robert. *Sound.* Scientific Magic. New York: Franklin Watts, 1992.

Lampton, Christopher F. *Sound: More Than What You Hear.* Hillside, NJ: Enslow Publishers, 1992.

Peacock, Graham. *Sound.* Science Activities. New York: Thomson Learning, 1993.

Pettigrew, Mark. *Music and Sound.* Science Today. New York: Gloucester Press, 1987.

Taylor, Barbara. *Sound.* Focus On. New York: Gloucester Press, 1992.

Taylor, Barbara. *Sound and Music.* Science Starters. New York: Franklin Watts, 1991.

Ward, Alan. *Experimenting With Sound.* New York: Chelsea House, 1991.

Wood, Robert W. *Forty-Nine Easy Experiments With Acoustics.* Blue Ridge Summit, PA: TAB Books, 1990.

INDEX

Air 6, 7
Alpine horn 12
Amplifier 15, 19, 26, 27, 28
Amplitude 9
Analog recording 27
Animals 5, 17, 18, 20, 21, 22

Birds 5, 18, 19, 20
Boyle, Robert 7

Cassette tape 27, 28
Communication 4, 19, 29
Compact disc 9, 27, 29
Computers 27, 28, 29

Deafness 14, 15
Decibels 9
Digital recording 27
Drum 6, 15

Ear 14, 17
  drum 14
  inner 14
  protectors 9
  shape 17
  trumpet 15, 16
Echoes 12, 20
Edison, Thomas 27
Explosions 11

Faraday, Michael 26
Foghorn 12
Frequency 8, 13, 19

Gases 7

Hearing
  aids 15
  damage 9
  sensitivity 17
Heartbeat 16

Insects 18

Lipreading 15
Liquids 7
Listening stick 16
Loudness 8, 9
Loudspeaker 6, 26, 27, 28

Mach
  Ernst 10
  numbers 10
Microphone 16, 28
Morse code 29
Music 9, 15, 22-25, 29
  instruments 23-25, 28
  notes 22, 25

Oersted, Hans Christian 26
Ornithologists 19

Percussion instruments 23
Personal stereo 9
Pitch 22, 25
  high 8, 9, 14, 20
  low 8, 14
Pollution 9

Radio 6, 26
Record 27
Recording studio 28
Reverberation 12
Rhythm 25
Rockets 7

Samplers 28
Sign language 15
Singing 13, 22
Solids 6, 7
Sonar 21
Sonic boom 10, 11
Sound
  cannon 11
  direction 14
  electronic 26
  energy 11, 13
  machines 4
  natural 4
  recording 27, 28
  reflection 12
  signals 29
  speed 10
  underwater 20
  warning 4
  waves 6, 14
Stereo system 15, 26
Stethoscope 16
String instruments 23
Synthesizers 26

Telephone 29
Television 9, 26
Thunderstorm 10

Ultrasound 20

Vibration 6, 7, 8, 9, 13, 14, 15, 20, 27
Volume 6, 9

Water 6, 21
Whistle 8
Wind instruments 23, 24